Bob Hartman's
Old Testament Tales
The Unauthorized Version

Now for the other side of the story!

The Bible version of the Old Testament tales may be the official one. But there were plenty of characters on the sidelines who saw things from a different angle.

Packed full of humour, mischief, silliness, and fun: these unauthorized versions from master storyteller Bob Hartman get to the heart of the matter.

Bob Hartman knows how to captivate an audience, and regularly entertains children and adults around the world as a performance storyteller. He is perhaps best known for the widely acclaimed *Lion Storyteller Bible*. When he is not writing, Bob enjoys making music, reading about classic cars, and entertaining his grandchildren.

Text copyright © 2012 Bob Hartman
This edition copyright © 2012 Lion Hudson

The moral rights of the author have been asserted

A Lion Children's Book
an imprint of
Lion Hudson plc
Wilkinson House, Jordan Hill Road,
Oxford OX2 8DR, England
www.lionhudson.com
ISBN 978 0 7459 6283 2 (print)
ISBN 978 0 7459 6725 7 (epub)
ISBN 978 0 7459 6724 0 (Kindle)
ISBN 978 0 7459 6726 4 (PDF)

First edition 2012
10 9 8 7 6 5 4 3 2 1 0
First electronic edition 2012

This book has been printed on paper and board independently certified
as having been produced from sustainable forests.

A catalogue record for this book is available
from the British Library

Typeset in 14/17 Baskerville MT Schoolbook
Printed and bound in Great Britain by Clays Ltd, St Ives plc

Distributed by:
UK: Marston Book Services Ltd, PO Box 269, Abingdon, Oxon
OX14 4YN
USA: Trafalgar Square Publishing, 814 N Franklin Street, Chicago,
IL 60610
USA Christian Market: Kregel Publications, PO Box 2607, Grand Rapids,
MI 49501

Bob Hartman's Old Testament Tales

THE UNAUTHORIZED VERSION

LION
CHILDREN'S

Contents

Introduction

Why "Unauthorized"?

Well, in 2011, the Authorized or King James Version of the Bible celebrated its 400th anniversary, and I thought that it might be fun to write an Unauthorized Version.

As "Authorized" suggests "official", "traditional", "approved of", I figured that an unauthorized version of the Bible stories would come from the point of view of sources that were not official or traditional. So I set about making up other voices to tell these familiar stories:

- a disgruntled soldier trying to knock down the walls of Jericho
- the Health and Safety Inspector at the battle between David and Goliath
- one of the lions in the den into which Daniel was dropped.

I tried to tell the stories in a way that would be true to the original, but also in a way that would bring out the humour in them.

I sort of doubt that anyone will be reading these in 400 years' time, but I hope that you enjoy them, and that you chuckle (at least a little). That will be approval enough for me.

Bob Hartman

Adam's Version

The Garden of Eden

"Right then, Adam," God announced. "I've got a job for you to do!"

"A job?" said Adam, lying on his back and sucking on a plum. "What's a job?"

"Erm… it's a task," God replied. "A work-related activity that requires a bit of effort and creativity on your part. Like when I made the world. Though on a much smaller scale."

"Hmm," Adam frowned, sucking the juice off his fingers and tossing the stone on the ground. "Not really sure I'm up for that. Creating stuff, I mean."

"It will be a different kind of creating," God explained. "I'll send animals your way, and all you have to do is make up names for them."

"Oh," said Adam, relieved. "That doesn't sound too difficult. Names for animals? Sure, why not? And you don't mind if I carry on lying here?"

"Not at all," God replied. "Though I suspect that you might find it necessary to move… eventually. Some of the animals are rather large."

"I'll keep that in mind," Adam shrugged, peeling a banana. "When do I start?"

"Immediately," said God. "Oh, and there's one other thing. You might like to keep an eye open for a helper. A companion."

"Got it," said Adam, chewing furiously. "Name the animals. Look for a helper. Anything else?"

"Just a suggestion," God replied. "You're meant to eat the inside of that fruit and throw the outside away. Not the other way round."

"I'll make a point of remembering that," said Adam, spitting out a mouthful of skin. "Ready when you are."

And as soon as he'd said it, a big fluffy creature bounded up to Adam, put its paws on his chest, and started licking his face.

"Enough! Enough!" cried Adam, pushing the animal away and leaping to his feet. Adam was afraid that the animal would be angry, but it just stood there, tongue hanging out and tail wagging. He could have sworn that it was smiling at him.

"Hmm," he muttered. "A name? Let's see. How about 'Happy Licky Waggy Thing'?"

And the animal made a noise. "Woof!"

"I'll take that as a 'yes'," Adam grinned. "Now go away, Happy Licky Waggy Thing. God is going to send me another animal."

But the Happy Licky Waggy Thing just stood there, wagging away.

"All right then," said Adam. "Stay if you'd rather. I don't mind. Maybe you're supposed to be my helper."

So the Happy Licky Waggy Thing stayed and watched with interest as several other animals paraded by.

"Right," said Adam. "I think I'll call you… hmm… 'Fluffy Snuffly Hoppy Thing'."

And the Happy Licky Waggy Thing went "woof" again.

"I'm glad you approve," Adam replied.

And so it went on. He named Snappy Scaly Thrashy Things, Beaky Pecky Clucky Things, Poky Shelly Lumpy Things, and Sting-y Stripy Buzzy Things.

And when God came to visit that evening, Adam was lying on the ground again, exhausted.

"This creating business is hard work," he sighed.

"Tell me about it," God replied. "I needed a rest when I was done. And you've barely started. Oh, and have you found a helper yet?"

"Nah," Adam sighed, struggling with a banana stem. "I thought that Happy Licky Waggy Thing might have been the one, but he's entirely too agreeable. I can't be getting all these names right – but he always acts the same. A wag and a woof. I think I need someone to challenge me. To keep me on my toes."

"Couldn't agree more," said God. "Oh, and there's an easier way to open that. Have a word with that creature above you there, in the tree."

"What? The Cheeky Jumpy Swingy Thing? Sure. Why not?"

So he chucked the banana in the air and the Cheeky Jumpy Swingy Thing grabbed it, turned it upside down, and snapped open the bottom of it with a flick of his thumb.

"Amazing!" thought Adam.

"Perhaps that's supposed to be my helper."

The next day was much the same. Adam named the animals, and the Happy Licky Waggy Thing woofed his approval. But the Cheeky Jumpy Swingy Thing was much harder to please. In fact, he screeched and chattered and shook his head at every one of Adam's suggestions.

"Growly Roary Tawny Thing?" said Adam.
Screech!

"Stinky Blacky Whitey Thing?" he offered.
Chatter!

"Spiky Curly Bally Thing?" he tried.
A shaking of the head!

And when God came to visit that evening, Adam was lying on the ground once more, frustrated AND exhausted.

"There's no pleasing that creature," he muttered, gnawing on the fuzzy shell of a coconut. "And THIS! Are you sure this is food?"

"One problem at a time," God sighed. "No, the Cheeky Jumpy Swingy Thing was not created to be your helper. And, yes, that thing you have in your hands is indeed meant to be eaten. But once again, the foody bit is on the inside."

"And how am I supposed to get at it?" grumbled Adam, banging it against his head.

"Throw it on the path over there… right… now!" said God.

CRUNCH!

So Adam did, just as a Trompy Stompy Trumpety Thing trundled by.

"No! Wait!" cried Adam, as a huge grey foot fell on his food. And then he smiled and said, "Oh yes, I see." And he picked himself up and picked over the pieces and picked out the soft white lumps from inside.

"MMM," Adam chewed. "That's good!"

"I couldn't have put it better myself," God agreed. "But the difficulty you're having getting at all the good food I made for you suggests that you might need that helper sooner rather than later."

"I don't mind looking a bit longer," Adam shrugged. "Actually I found a very nice Milky Mooey Patchy Thing today. Could that be my helper?"

"Don't think so," God replied.

"The Quacky Splishy Webby Thing?"

"Again – no."

"How about that Baby Scratchy Meowy Thing?"

"And what help would that be?" asked God.

"Don't know, but it's so cute," grinned Adam. "With its big brown eyes and its cuddly little paws."

"Don't be ridiculous," God sighed. "It'll only grow up into a cat. No, I think your helper needs to be tailor-made. Go to sleep, and in the morning you will find what you have been looking for."

So Adam went to sleep. And while he slept, God took a rib from Adam's side. And out of that rib,

God made Adam a helper.

The next morning, Adam named the animals again, with the Happy Licky Waggy Thing on his left side and the Cheeky Jumpy Swingy Thing on the right. "I think we should call that a Longy Stretchy Necky thing," he suggested.

Happy Licky Waggy Thing woofed. Cheeky Jumpy Swingy Thing screeched.

And then a voice from behind them said, "I like the Stretchy Necky bit. But I think the Longy bit is a little repetitive. What about SPOTTY Stretchy Necky Thing?"

"That's not bad," agreed Adam. "Not bad at all."

And then he stopped and a shiver went up his spine. It wasn't God who was talking, and it wasn't one of the animals either. Slowly he turned around. And his animal friends did the same.

Happy Licky Waggy Thing went, "Woof!" Cheeky Jumpy Swingy Thing leaped up and down excitedly.

And Adam just went, "Wow!"

"Excellent name," God chuckled. "And I have the sneaking feeling that generations of men to follow will choose the same one. But I have decided to call her 'Eve'. Adam, meet your helper!"

"Pleased to meet you, Eve." Adam smiled.

"The pleasure is mine." Eve smiled in return.

"Would you like to name some more animals?" asked Adam.

"I'd love to," Eve replied. "But I'm feeling a little hungry. I don't suppose we could eat that thing over there?" she asked, pointing at a melon.

"I've had a bit of a problem with those," Adam confessed. "I've licked them and I've gnawed them, and frankly they don't taste very good."

"Perhaps the foody bit is inside, somehow," Eve suggested, picking up a rock. "What if we whack it and crack it open?"

"I think that might help," Adam nodded. "That's a great idea!"

"I think it might," God agreed. And Eve set about whacking the melon.

"So what do you think of your helper?" God whispered to Adam.

"She's perfect," Adam replied. "Everything is just perfect now."

"Perfect," God mused. "Hmm. That's exactly what I was going to say."

The Shepherd Boy's Version

Moses and the Burning Bush

The shepherd boy slumped down beside his bigger shepherd brother. "You'll never guess what I just saw," he said.

"Sheep?" suggested his brother sarcastically.

"No," he replied. "I saw a bush."

The older brother surveyed the barren landscape. "Now that is news," he said, just a fraction less sarcastically. "Perhaps we should tell the sheep. They'd love a nice bush to chomp on."

"It wasn't an ordinary bush," the shepherd boy added.

"A special bush then?" sniggered his brother. "Dripping with honey, was it? Covered in jewels? The sheep will be pleased."

"Stop it!" glared the shepherd boy. "This is serious. The bush was on fire!"

"That is serious," his brother agreed with a smirk. "But not what I'd call special. There is this little thing called lightning, you see…"

"I know about lightning," the shepherd boy sighed. "And there wasn't a cloud in the sky. Anyway, that's not the special thing. The special thing is that the bush was on fire, but the bush wasn't burning up!"

"Really?" said the older brother sceptically.

"I swear! Honest!" said the shepherd boy.

"And you watched this burning, not-burning bush for how long…?"

"For ages!" insisted the shepherd boy. "I couldn't take my eyes off it. And not one of the leaves was burned. I promise."

"Mmm-hmm," nodded the older brother. "I've heard of those bushes. Distantly related to the smouldering dandelion and the heat-resistant hyacinth, I believe."

"It's not funny!" shouted the shepherd boy.

"Oh yes, it is," grinned his brother. "You have no idea." Then he plucked something from the ground. "And look, here's a slightly singed blade of grass. Result!"

"You can laugh all you want," the shepherd boy sulked. "Moses was there and he saw it, too."

"Moses?" replied his brother. "Crotchety old Moses – the shepherd who lives on the other side of the mountain? Mildly Mad Moses who is always mumbling to himself? That Moses?"

"It's just the way he speaks," the shepherd boy muttered.

"Oh, so you've met him then?" asked his older brother. "I didn't realize you'd had the pleasure. You know they say he killed somebody once?"

"I didn't meet him," the shepherd boy explained. "I sort of ran away when he arrived, because, yeah… well… I heard he'd killed somebody once. And I hid behind a boulder."

"Was the boulder on fire, too?" inquired his older brother.

"No! Of course not! Stop it!" shouted the shepherd boy.

The older brother tapped his chin with his forefinger, thinking. "So if you didn't meet Moses," he asked, "how do you know the way he speaks?"

The shepherd boy said nothing for a bit. He just looked at the ground. "If I tell you," he muttered, "you'll think I'm crazy."

"We passed that point some time ago," said his brother. "Try me."

"I know what he sounds like because I heard

him… talking… to… the bush."

"Mildly Mad Moses," the older brother shrugged. "What did I say? The name fits. Now if YOU had been talking to the bush, that would have been different. Or if the bush had talked back…"

The shepherd boy turned his head, looked at his brother, smiled sheepishly, and raised one eyebrow.

"Please don't tell me that the bush talked back," said his brother.

"The bush talked back," whispered the shepherd boy. "Actually, to be fair, it was the bush that sort

of started the conversation."

"Mmm-hmm," the older brother nodded again. "And what did the bush say? Let me guess. 'Do you have any water? I'm on fire!' maybe. Or 'I could do with a trim.' Put me out of my misery, please! What did the bush say?"

"'Moses'," said the shepherd boy. "It said, 'Moses, Moses.' And when Moses said 'Here I am!', the bush told him to take off his sandals."

"That would not have been my first guess," his brother smirked.

"It's not funny," said the shepherd boy. "It was really scary! I took off my sandals, too, just in case."

"Just in case what?" asked his brother.

"In case the god in the bush got really angry with me."

"Oh, now there's a GOD in the bush?" said his brother. "That explains everything! You were in the presence of some sacred bit of shrubbery. Does this god have a name?"

"Not exactly," said the shepherd boy. "He told Moses that he was the god of Abraham, Isaac, and Jacob."

"Who are…?"

"Moses' ancestors, apparently," the shepherd boy shrugged.

"Never heard of them," his brother shrugged back.

"Well, according to the bush…" the shepherd boy went on.

"Plant life being the obvious go-to source of information about one's ancestors," his brother chuckled.

"According to the GOD in the bush," the shepherd boy continued, "they are the ancestors of the Israelites – some group of people who are slaves in Egypt. And this god is their god, and he spoke from the bush to tell Moses that he had been chosen by the god in the bush to set those people free."

The older brother paused and scratched his head.

"So these people are slaves in Egypt?"

"Yes."

"The greatest empire the world has ever seen."

"Yep."

"And this god wants Moses to set them free?"

"That's right."

"Mildly Mad Moses?"

"Uh-huh."

"Who lives on the other side of the mountain."

"Yup."

"Who is a shepherd just like us?"

"Exactly."

"Who can't put a sentence together without stumbling?"

"Apparently."

Again the shepherd boy's brother paused. And then he spoke. "The bush didn't give off any smoke by any chance, did it? Deprived you of oxygen? Left you slightly confused…?"

"NO!" the shepherd boy insisted. "That is exactly what the bush – the GOD in the bush – said. Why would I make it up? How could I make it up?"

His brother nodded. "You have a point there. So what happened next? I'm curious. How exactly is Moses supposed to set these people free?"

"The god in the bush said he'd help Moses," the shepherd boy explained. "And he showed him how to do these miracles – turning a stick into a snake, making his hand all horrible and diseased-looking. And there was something about turning Nile water into blood. It was pretty amazing. Oh, and he said something about Moses having a brother who could do all the speaking for him. Sounds like the god had worked it all out."

"Sounds more like Moses is about to get himself killed," the shepherd's brother said. "Doesn't sound very promising to me."

"I wonder," mused the shepherd boy. "I mean, if this god can make a bush burn – and not burn – and do the miracles I saw, maybe he really can set those people free."

His brother shrugged. "I guess we'll just have to wait and see. I do like that bit about Moses' brother, though. They can be very useful, brothers. And hopefully, Moses' brother will be as helpful as I have been."

"You haven't been helpful at all," sighed the shepherd boy. "You've just poked fun at everything I've said."

"Which is what Moses' brother should do, if he has any sense. And then maybe Moses will forget about the bush, or the god in the bush, or whatever it is, and save himself a lot of trouble."

"So should we go and warn him or something?" asked the shepherd boy.

"What? Moses?" replied his brother. "Are you kidding? They say he killed somebody. No, let his own brother sort him out. I say we go home. I might be wrong, but I thought I heard Mum calling for us."

"Really?" said the shepherd boy.

"Sorry," grinned his brother. "My mistake. It was that olive tree over there."

The Donkey's Version

Balaam's Donkey

When my master told me that we had an important visitor staying, I paid no attention. We'd had plenty of important visitors before.

But when he told me who it was and what I was supposed to do, I could hardly contain my excitement.

"Are you sure you want me to take care of her?" I asked. "There are plenty of older servants who would give anything for this chance."

"No," said my master. "You're just a boy, I know, but I think there is much you can learn from this guest. And also," he added, "being young, you are perhaps more – shall we say – open to unusual things. Things that the others would find just a little disturbing."

I have to admit that I was nervous when I first met her. I'd heard that the first few moments with her could be a bit of a shock. Those lips and that tongue forming those words.

She was smaller than I thought she would be, but she was beautifully groomed. Her mane was black and trimmed short. And her grey coat was brushed perfectly.

"So you must be my servant boy," she said. And with a shake of her head, the donkey motioned for me to come closer.

It was a shock. To see her speak. And I think she knew how I was feeling.

"Why don't I tell you my story?" she suggested. "To put you at ease. And then you can fetch me a drink."

"All right," I nodded. It was exactly what I wanted to hear.

And she cleared her throat with a bray and a snort. "I was an ordinary donkey," she began. "The property of my master, Balaam. In those days, he was quite a popular figure. A mystical, magical man, who put curses on people for a fee."

"And they worked? These curses?" I asked.

"Amazingly, yes," she grinned. "But then you're sitting here, talking to a donkey – so maybe you wouldn't find that so amazing after all.

"It was small stuff at first. Stopping cows from giving milk, chickens from laying eggs, sheep from giving birth. But as his reputation grew, so the jobs got bigger. And that's how we found ourselves on the way to a meeting with the kings of Midian and Moab."

"So you were with him from the start?" I asked.

"Oh yes," she nodded. "But it's not as if I had a choice. Not like today. I belonged to him. He had a whip. I carried him where he told me to go."

"And the kings?"

"The kings wanted him to put a curse on an entire nation," she continued. "The Israelites. We were off to seal the deal, but we ran into a little 'trouble' on the way."

"Bandits?" I asked. "Bad weather? Bad roads?"

"An angel," she whispered. And she smiled when she saw the look on my face.

"You're talking to a donkey," she reminded me. "How strange is an angel compared to that?" She had a point.

"So what did the angel do?"

"He tried to stop us," the donkey shrugged again. "He appeared out of nowhere in front of me, a drawn sword in his hand. And I did what any sensible donkey would do. I turned off the road and into a nearby field."

"And what did Balaam do?" I asked.

"He beat me with his whip." And I could see the hurt in her eyes.

"I have to admit, I was surprised," she continued. "Not by the beating. Balaam was not a patient man. No, what surprised me was his – how shall I put it? – ingratitude. I had just, as far as I could tell, saved his magical, mystical skin. And the whip was my reward."

"And you told him so?" I suggested.

"I said nothing at that moment. Not a hee. Not a haw. I simply turned back on to the road, by which time the angel had disappeared.

"I confess to having had a moment or two of doubt. Had the angel really been there? Had I perhaps been imagining things? It was a hot day, to be fair, and heat can do strange things to a donkey with a load on her back.

"Eventually, the road passed through a vineyard. There was a wall on one side and a wall on the other, with the road narrowing in between. And that's when the angel appeared again."

"So you couldn't turn off?"

"Precisely. The best I could do was to press up against one wall. And as I did so, I inadvertently crushed Balaam's foot against it."

She smiled. "It did seem like a just reward for the beating. But then he beat me again, and I decided that 'tit-for-tat' with a man and his whip was not the smartest game I could play.

"And – before you ask – no, I did not tell him off at that moment either.

"The road continued to narrow, the walls pressing in on both sides. And when we reached the point where there was no longer enough room to turn, the angel appeared for the third time.

"I had run out of options, to be honest. So I did what donkeys do when they reach that point: I dropped to my knees and refused to move any further."

"And Balaam…?"

"Oh, he beat me again. Beat me for all he was worth. Cursing and complaining and rueing the day he'd bought me.

"And, yes, that was the moment I opened my mouth and spoke. 'What have I done?' I asked. 'To deserve three beatings?'"

"He must have been shocked," I said. "When he heard those words come from your mouth."

She grinned. "That's the interesting thing. He was so angry that I don't think he noticed at all. He just carried on ranting: 'You've made a fool of me! …

I'll miss my appointment! … If I had a sword, I'd kill you!'

"So I ranted back, 'Am I not your donkey? … Don't you trust me? … Have I ever behaved this way before?'

"We were like some old married couple, arguing about our years together. I swear I heard the angel chuckle. But when he followed that by clearing his throat, everything changed.

"Balaam looked up and trembled and then bowed down. And it was clear that this was the first time he'd seen what was really going on."

"So the angel had been invisible to him?" I asked.

"It must have been," she answered. "An honest mistake on the part of the angel, I suppose. But it didn't take away the sting of those three beatings – a point that the angel proceeded to make on my behalf.

"Why did you beat your donkey?" he asked Balaam. "I came to stop you because you are travelling along a reckless path. Your donkey saw me and turned away. If she hadn't, I would certainly have killed you. Killed you and spared her."

"So did Balaam apologize to you?" I asked.

And she snorted – the biggest and longest snort so far.

"Not likely. No, he was too busy saving his magical, mystical skin. He apologized to the angel, of course. And promised to go back home straightaway. But that's not what the angel wanted."

"No?" I asked, curious.

"No, the angel had obviously been sent by the God of the Israelites. And he had something he wanted Balaam to do.

"'Go and meet the kings,' the angel said. 'But only say what I tell you to.'"

"So you went to see the kings?"

"We went to see the kings. And that's when everything became clear. Every time they asked my

master to curse the people of Israel, he blessed them instead. It was funny. At least, I thought so. I tried to explain it all to the king's horses, but they just stood there and ignored me."

"Because you were talking like a human?" I asked.

"No," she brayed. "Because horses are stuck-up. I thought everybody knew that."

"Sorry," I apologized. "I didn't…"

"Not to worry," she hee-hawed. "Anything else you'd like to know?"

"Are you still in touch with Balaam?" I asked.

And she shook her head. "It was difficult after that. He had trouble getting work. As you can imagine, no one trusted him. My reputation, however, just kept on growing. You'd be amazed at how many people want to see a talking donkey."

"So Balaam set you free?"

And she threw back her head and laughed, a mouthful of teeth on show. "Set me free? I left! What did I need him for? A man with a whip? Puh-lease!

"And now I talk. People listen. If you must know, I'm the one who cracks the whip. Well, not literally – I couldn't hold one if I wanted to. But when I want something, all I have to do is stamp my hoof and it's there. I couldn't ask for more."

And then she laughed again. "Well, of course, I could ask – that's the point, isn't it? I'm a talking donkey."

"So do you ever hear from him then?"

And there was just the slightest hint of sadness in her eyes. "I didn't for a long while. And then, just last week, I received word that my former master is dead."

"No!"

"Yes. Seems as if he was desperate for work – any work. So he hooked up with the king of Moab again and was killed in battle – by the Israelites. Ironic, isn't it? All that angelic warning gone to waste.

"Didn't do me any harm, though, did it? And, on reflection, it does make me wonder: who was the real donkey after all?"

And with a stamp of her hoof, the story was over and the time for serving had begun.

"Now, how about that drink?" she brayed.

The Soldier's Version

The Battle of Jericho

"So how was work today?" I asked my dad. And he slammed his helmet on the table.

"Not good," he grunted. "Not good at all.

"I showed up on time at the walls of Jericho, ready for a day of killing and maiming. And then the priests arrived."

"Priests?" asked my mum. She was making dinner. Goat stew. "Why priests?"

"Some special secret plan," he sighed again. "That only Joshua, our commander, knows. It was like a parade. The priests went first. Then the guys on the ram's horn trumpets. Then the ark of the covenant."

"Ark of the covenant?" I said.

"Yeah, you know – the sacred box with the Ten Commandments inside," said my dad.

"So where were you?" asked my mum.

"Behind the ark," grumbled my dad.

"And the battering rams?" I asked excitedly. "Where were the battering rams?"

"Battering rams?" he scoffed. "There weren't any battering rams! I spoke to my mate Dave, who is second in command in the Battering Ram Division, and he told me that they'd been given the day off! Apparently, they had organized a picnic and they spent the day at a place of scenic beauty."

"Sounds lovely," nodded my mum.

"Not if you're trying to knock down a wall!" my dad shouted.

"So did you knock it down?" I asked.

"No, we didn't. We marched around the city. Once. The priests blew their trumpets. And then we went home. A right waste of time."

"Never mind, dear," said my

mum, spooning out the stew. "Eat your dinner. I'm sure things will be better tomorrow."

As it happens, things weren't.

"I'm raring to go!" he announced the next morning. "Itching to skewer a resident of Jericho – or two."

But when he got home from work that night, he was even more frustrated. And he was still itching.

"Flippin' fleas!" he moaned, slapping himself around the shoulders. "I spent the day fighting these things off. And that's all I fought!"

"So no battle then?" asked my mum. She was making dinner. Goat stew.

"No," he grumbled. "We just marched around the walls again. More priests and trumpets – and the ark, of course."

"And battering rams?" I asked hopefully.

Dad rolled his eyes. "Field trip, apparently. A bit of bird-watching. Some flower-gathering. That's what my mate Dave told me."

"So nothing got crushed?" I said.

And he squeezed a flea between his fingers. "Nothing but these blinkin' insects. And what's worse, the people of Jericho were laughing at us! They think this is some kind of joke."

"Maybe it's a clever plan," I suggested. "So they let their guard down for when you finally attack."

"IF we attack," he groaned.

"Never mind, dear," said my mum. "Here's your stew. Perhaps things will be better tomorrow."

But the next day was even worse.

"Don't ask!" shouted my dad, storming into our tent.

So we didn't. But it didn't help.

"I was desperate to destroy something!" he shouted again. "All we did was march around the city. Priests! Trumpets! Ark! And before anyone says it, the Battering Ram Division went to see a show!"

"A show?" asked my mum. She was making dinner. Goat stew.

"At the other end of the camp," he grunted. "There's a man with a monkey. He juggles, apparently.

"What, the monkey?" I asked.

"No, the man. I don't know! And I don't care! I just wanted to kill something. Not march around after a bunch of... of... trumpet-toting tabernacle attendants."

"Now that's a bit harsh, dear," tutted my mum. "My friend Betty heard them the other day and she said they were very good. There's a short beardy one on the end who is sometimes out of tune, but she reckons that the rest make a really nice sound. She told me that some of the people of Jericho even clapped. I think that says it all."

"They clapped because they're still alive!" cried

my dad. "If we were doing our job, they'd be screaming for mercy."

"I think someone needs to calm down, dear," she suggested. "Have some stew. I'm sure they'll let you dismember someone tomorrow."

When my dad got home the next day, he was cursing and scraping his helmet with a stick.

"Can't get the cheese off," he muttered.

"Cheesed off again, are we dear?" called my mum. She was making dinner. Goat stew.

"No!" he shouted. "Well, yes. What I said was, 'I can't get the cheese off.'"

She looked up from the cooking pot. "And why would there be cheese on your helmet, dear?" she asked. 'Did you murder a bit of gorgonzola today?'

"I wish I'd murdered something!" And then he sighed. "The truth is, I was late reporting for duty this morning."

My mum gasped. My dad was a good soldier. He was never late.

"I just didn't see the point," he explained. "Marching around that blasted city again."

"Did you get into trouble?" I asked.

"No. My sergeant is just as fed up as I am. But there was trouble, trust me. And this stinking cheese is the proof!

"Up until now, I have never marched with the soldiers at the very back. But if you get there late, that's where you go. And I had no idea of the kind of abuse they were getting from the people of Jericho."

"What kind?" I asked.

"They throw things," said my dad. "Sticks and stones at first. Fair enough. But then they chucked their rubbish at us. Pigs' trotters. Chicken beaks. Dog bones. You name it."

"Cheese?" guessed my mum.

"Buckets of the stuff," grunted my dad. "And really smelly, too."

I shuddered. "That must have been horrible."

"Nowhere near as horrible as what we'll do to them when we get inside that wall," he promised.

"And the Battering Ram Division?" asked mum.

"Manicures," muttered my dad, scraping away at his helmet. "And would you look at that? I just broke a nail. Typical."

My mum pushed a bowl in his direction. "Stew, dear. In your own time."

"Humiliating." That's all my dad said when he walked into the tent the next day.

"Did you lose your battle, dear?"

asked my mum. She was cooking dinner. Goat stew.

"What battle?" he grumbled. "There was no battle! Just another little march around the city."

"Priests," said my mum.

"Trumpets," I added.

"You've got the idea," my dad nodded.

"And the Battering Ram Division?" I asked.

"Making models," he sighed. "Though, to be fair, they were models of battering rams."

"That sounds good," said my mum.

"No," replied my dad, "because we're not DOING anything. And the people of Jericho just aren't afraid of us at all. In fact, today they even called us chickens."

"I think that's rather sweet," said my mum. "I have always found chickens to be delightful creatures with their cheery little clucks and that jaunty strutting gait. Now, goats, on the other hand –"

"It's an insult!" shouted my dad, flapping his arms and jerking his head about.

"Well, when you do it that way," replied my mum, "I can see what you mean. That's not attractive at all."

"It's an insult because they are saying that we are cowards!" he shouted again.

"I don't follow," she went on. "Corner a chicken and you are in for the fight of your life. Why, my own mother was pursued around the yard on more than one occasion by a pack of poultry. It took her years to recover. In fact, she still –"

"I don't care!" cried my dad. "It's an insult!"

"Maybe it's a warning," I suggested. "Maybe what they're saying is that there are giant chickens inside the walls, ready to crush you when you break through."

"A very good theory," nodded my mum. "See, dear, we both think that you are taking this far too personally. The people of Jericho were obviously saying that you are fierce and brave and to be feared."

"And a little jaunty," I added.

Dad shook his head. "I don't know…"

"Why don't you have a lie-down?" she suggested. "The stew will still be here when you wake up."

"Maybe I should," he muttered, trudging off.

As soon as he'd left, I looked at my mum. "I don't think he's a chicken," I said.

"No," she replied with a wink. "Bravest man I know. But he does struggle a bit with self-esteem."

When my dad came home from work the next night, he had a fierce and determined look in his eye. "Tomorrow!" he announced. "Tomorrow I am going to get to the bottom of this. Tomorrow is going to be different!"

"And why is that, dear?" asked my mum. She was making dinner. Goat stew.

"Because tomorrow my mate Dave is going to ask his boss to talk to Joshua – and then we're going to find out who came up with this crazy plan in the first place!"

"Your mate Dave in the Battering Ram Division?" I asked.

"Who spent the day in the hot springs at the other end of the camp," he sighed.

"While you marched around the city?" added my mum.

"I have stopped caring," he replied. "But tomorrow everything will be different. Because tomorrow, at least I will know who's responsible. And then… and then… I don't know – maybe somehow I'll be able to change things. Take control. Do something other than march around walls and eat goat stew every day!"

I thought for a moment that my mum was going to cry. But she held back the tears and replied quietly, "It's a very big goat."

My dad opened the tent flap and had a look.

"I'm sorry, darling," he whispered. "You're right. And it appears that we still have three legs to go. My apologies."

And so it was that when my dad came home that seventh day, things were indeed different.

He was grinning from ear to ear. "You'll never guess," he began.

"Oh, I think I can, dear," my mum smiled.

"We won the battle of course," he went on. "Jericho is finally ours. But the plan…"

"Was it Dave's?" I asked.

And he laughed. "No, Dave and the Battering Ram Division were in the hills picking fruit."

I was confused. "Then how did you knock down the walls?"

"Didn't have to," he chuckled. "Because the plan wasn't Dave's. It wasn't any of the commanders'. And it wasn't even Joshua's."

"Then whose plan was it, dear?" asked my mum.

"God's," he answered. "That's what Dave's boss told him anyway. And God's plan was that we should march around the city for six days in a row, blowing our trumpets, etcetera. And then, on the seventh day, that we should march around seven times, blow one long trumpet note, and give a shout. And that if we did that, the walls would just fall down."

"Which they did?" I asked.

"Which they did!" he grinned. "And then of course there was all the fighting and mopping up to do."

"So God had it under control the whole time, dear," said my mum. "All that complaining for nothing then."

"Yes, well…" he muttered. "The point is that we won."

"And that things are different now," she added, dishing out the dinner.

"Really?" he said, looking hopefully into his bowl.

"You can't expect to win every battle," she winked. "Now eat your goat stew, dear."

And he did.

The Detective's Version

Gideon and the Statue of Baal

It was midnight. The moon was full, but there were still shadows in the mean streets of Ophrah.

It had been a happy town, once. But then the Midianites had invaded, killing livestock, burning crops, and spreading fear.

I was working late, and that's why I saw it – a lone dark figure, creeping past my window as if he had something to hide.

I leaped to my feet, dagger in hand, and rushed to the door. But when I opened it, he was gone. So I stumbled into bed. But I did not sleep well. Not at all.

The name's Spade, by the way. Shemuel Spade. My business? Solving other people's problems.

I woke early the next morning. Someone was banging on the door.

I stumbled across the room. But when I opened the door, the sun blinded me for a moment, and I struggled to see who was there. Shadows again. The dark shadows of Ophrah. So I reached once more for my dagger.

"Hiya Shemuel!" the shadow said. And I put the dagger away. It was Ham, my errand boy and sometime assistant.

"How ya doing, kid?" I replied. And he really was a kid. Nine, maybe ten. I don't know. But he had a way with mysteries.

"Did you hear what happened?" he asked. And I shook my head.

"Sorry, kid," I grunted. "Rough night."

"It was a rough night in Ophrah, too," he announced. "You know that statue of Baal in the middle of town?"

I nodded. Don't have much time for religion, but if I want to worship a god, it will be the god of my own people – the God of Israel. Not some Midianite idol like Baal.

"Well, you'll never guess what happened," Ham went on. "Somebody knocked it down! Then they used the pieces to build an altar, and they sacrificed a bull on it.

"The people in the town who worship Baal are hopping mad. And everybody else is afraid that when the Midianites find out, they'll come looking for revenge. The town elders are on their way here to see if you can figure out who did it."

I smiled. Just a little. The elders had faith in me. I liked that. And I smiled for another reason, too. That shadow – the one who'd crept past my door in the night – I bet he had something to do with this. I was already on the case.

The town elders told me pretty much the same thing that the boy had. None of them had a clue who the culprit was. So I said goodbye and made my way to the scene of the crime.

Ophrah can be a tough town, but there were plenty of tears when I got to the altar. Baal-worshippers. Frightened citizens. And old Joash, who owned the burned-up bull.

"What a mess," I grunted.

And Ham just nodded.

I interviewed anyone who would talk to me, but nobody had seen anything. "The middle of the night." That's all anyone said. And I couldn't get the picture of that mysterious stranger out of my head.

The boy tapped me on the back. "Have you seen this?" he asked. And he pointed to the ground.

Sure enough, there was a footprint – a single,
purple footprint – on a stone slab.

"What do you think it means?" he asked.

And I shook my head. "Don't know. Might belong

to the perpetrator. But why is it purple? And why is there only one?"

Visions of a hideous, hopping, purple-footed fiend filled my mind. And I wracked my brains to remember – had that mysterious stranger moved on two feet or one?

"Maybe he just put one foot on the slab," suggested Ham. "And the next one landed in the dirt."

It was an explanation that had some merit. It was sorely lacking in drama, though.

"No, we're looking for a one-footed man," I said. "Or someone who goes about on one foot. A hopper."

"But I don't think there's anybody like that in town," the boy replied. "And why would he leave a purple stain behind?"

The boy was eager, but lacking in experience.

"Obviously he came from another town," I explained. "That's why we've never seen him before. As for the purple stain, I think that maybe he comes from a town where they paint themselves purple. A purple hopping person from a purple hopping town. Where they hate Baals and bulls and Midianites. Find that town and we find our man."

I grinned. That was my first guess. And my first guesses were almost always right.

Ham scratched his head. "But I've never heard

of a purple hopping town. Couldn't it be something simpler? Couldn't he have just – I don't know – stepped in something purple?"

I patted the boy on the head with an understanding smile. I'd been young once. And innocent. How could I explain to him that the world was a complicated place?

"You go and look for your purple puddle," I humoured him. "And I'll ask around about that hopping town. See you later, kid." And we went our separate ways.

He caught up with me a couple of hours later.

"I think I've found something!" he said excitedly.

"Calm down, kid," I replied. "Let's have it, one step at a time."

"I remembered what you said about the puddle," he began. And I couldn't help but chuckle. The kid didn't even get the joke.

"So I asked myself," he went on, "where I could find a purple puddle? And it came to me right away. In a wine press! That's where people squish the juice out of grapes, yeah? So I went to the wine press."

I shook my head. "Sorry to disappoint you, kid, but there must be dozens of people who have used that wine press. There's no way we can narrow it down to one. And besides, I just talked with someone who has a cousin who lives in a bouncing town. And where there are bouncers, there must be hoppers…"

But the kid ignored me. He wouldn't let go of the wine press thing.

"I thought of that," he continued. "But for the print to be left behind, the person's foot would have had to have been wet. Which means he would have been in the wine press the same day the statue got wrecked."

"That's a fair assumption," I nodded.

"And the only person anybody could remember seeing near the wine press that day," he concluded, "was Gideon, the son of Joash."

It was all I could do not to laugh.

"Hang on, kid," I said. "Two problems here. One, the burned-up bull belonged to Gideon's father. Two, Gideon is just about the biggest coward this town has ever seen. He wouldn't say 'boo' to a goose. He wouldn't get close enough to a goose so the goose would hear him say 'boo'. He'd hide somewhere the goose would never find him and not even bother saying 'boo' in the first place."

"Somewhere like a wine press maybe?" the boy asked.

"We're not talking about geese here!" I reminded him. "We're talking about tearing down a foreign idol and setting fire to livestock and making people really angry! People who will then show up at your door and do painful things to you. Gideon is the last person who would dare to do that."

"Maybe so," said Ham. "But he might be the first person to hide in a wine press! I don't see how it could hurt to talk to him."

The kid was stubborn. I liked that. Reminded me a bit of me. But I didn't think it would do him any harm to see how wrong-headed his little theory was. So I nodded my head and off we went.

When we arrived at Gideon's house, the kid got all excited again.

"Look! Look!" he shouted, pointing to another rocky slab. "A purple footprint, just like the first one! And did you see this? Bits of grain or something stuck to it."

"Calm down," I cautioned him. "It might be a coincidence. Or maybe that purple hopping town has sent a load of spies our way."

"But I can prove it's the same," he insisted. And he held up a broken stick.

"I used this to measure the first footprint," he explained. Then he laid it beside the new print and started shouting again. "It matches! It's the same length! Look!"

I was about to suggest the possibility of purple hopping twins when the door flew open and old Joash started shouting as well. "What's going on here? What do you want? Have you found that bull-burner yet?"

I shook my head. "No, but the boy here has this crazy notion that it was your son, Gideon. Claims he can match the footprint on your doorstep to the one at the scene of the crime."

And that's when the blubbering started. "I'm sorry, Father! I should have told you. I can explain, honest."

It was Gideon, weeping like a baby.

I looked at Ham and he just smiled.

"Beginner's luck," I thought. But I didn't say it. I just smiled back with a "Well done, kid."

And then it all came out. Seems that Gideon had been hiding in the wine press, threshing wheat in one corner, so the Midianites couldn't steal it. An angel appeared to him (I've heard stranger alibis) and told him that the God of Israel had chosen him to defeat the Midianites. And that, as his first act, he was to tear down the statue of Baal and sacrifice a bull to the God of Israel on the ruins.

It was the craziest story I'd ever heard. God choosing the biggest coward in town to defeat a whole army of invaders. Really? But his father bought it. And so did everybody else in Ophrah.

They wanted to kill him at first, but then his father said, "If Baal was a real god, why didn't he stop Gideon from tearing down the statue?"

Fair point, that. And they let Gideon go. Even gave him a nickname – Jerubbaal – which means something like "let Baal save himself".

Case closed then? Not quite. Gideon claimed he never walked past my house that night, and I never did discover who the mysterious moonlight stranger was.

So I went home and locked my door. Then, with my dagger at my side, I fell into an uneasy sleep.

And dreamed. Of the mean streets of Ophrah. And hoppers...

The Official Version

David and Goliath

When my mum told me that I was going to be apprenticed to her brother in the Israelite army, I thought that I would learn how to be a soldier.

I could not have been more wrong.

"There are two ways to get ahead in this man's army," he told me the very first morning. "Kill as many of the enemy as possible. Or work your bottom off to make things run more efficiently."

I looked at my uncle. He couldn't have weighed more than fifty kilos. And he wasn't even carrying a sword. It didn't take a genius to figure out that his job had to do with option number two. And so, now, did mine.

He handed me a soft clay tablet and a stylus. "You might want to take notes." he suggested.

"I am responsible for two areas, as far as the army of Israel is concerned," he began. "The first has to do with the general well-being of the soldiers. Keeping them fit and making sure that there is as little illness as possible."

"Health, then," I wrote on my tablet.

"My job is also to protect them from any unnecessary accidents," he went on. "You may think a battlefield is dangerous. But you would be surprised at the number of injuries that are sustained behind the lines. Tripping over misplaced shields. Falling onto badly positioned spears. I've seen it all. And it is my job to keep such incidents to a minimum."

"Safety, then," I wrote on my tablet. "Health. And Safety."

"I couldn't have put it better myself," my uncle grinned. "You learn quickly, boy. A bit like me, even if I say so myself. You'll have no trouble getting ahead."

Then he took me on his morning inspection.

"Who does this helmet belong to?" he asked. "It needs to be picked up and put in its place. Helmet accidents account for 15 per cent of injuries in the average battalion. And this sandal? Who left this sandal here? Someone could trip and fall."

He went on like this for an hour – shouting out violations and listing them on his own tablet as he went. The strange thing was that none of the soldiers seemed to pay him any attention.

"Yes, I know," he said when I asked. "It's quite normal for them to swear and spit on the ground when I point out their errors. No one likes to be criticized. And, speaking of criticism," he added, interrupting himself, "what is that boy doing here?"

There was, indeed, a boy. About ten years old, maybe eleven. And he was carrying bread and cheese.

"You there!" my uncle shouted. "Who are you and what are you doing here?"

"His name's David," grunted a soldier nearby. "He's a shepherd. And he's also my brother."

"And mine," grunted the soldier next to him.

"And mine, too," a third soldier chimed in.

"You're all his brothers?" my uncle asked.

And three heads nodded in unison.

"Well, he's too young to serve in the army," said my uncle. "And his presence here is a potential danger to you, as well as to himself. This is no place for a child!"

"But he's brought our lunch," the first brother replied.

"Ah, yes, lunch," noted my uncle, eyeballing the bread and cheese. Then he scribbled something on his tablet and continued.

"So where was this cheese produced? And what about the bread? Were work surfaces clean? Was the milk fresh? Was the flour free of bacteria?"

The soldier brothers looked at one another, confused.

"Dunno," one of them answered. "It came from our family's farm, I think."

"Ah, the family farm, " my uncle sighed, scribbling on his tablet again. "The most common source of disease in this man's army. No inspections. No certificates. Just good old mum and dad and their unwashed hands and germ-filled bowls and spoons."

Then he turned to the boy and reached for the cheese. "I'm afraid I'm going to have to take that," he said.

At once, three enormous soldier-brothers moved around us, in a circle.

"It's our lunch," the first brother repeated. And he said it as if he meant it. As if he might just eat us instead.

"Yes, well…" my uncle replied, sizing up the situation. "Perhaps I can let you off with a warning just this once. But you will be required to attend a course on soldierly hygiene. I'll expect you all at my tent next Monday. Ten o'clock sharp!"

The circle opened. We retreated. But my uncle didn't act as if it had been a retreat at all.

"A bit of give and take," he whispered to me as we hurried away. "That's what you need if you want to get ahead in this man's army."

"But it seems as if we did all the giving and they did all the taking," I replied.

"It may look that way," he grinned. "But we have sown a seed, challenged the way they think.

And that hygiene course? It lasts for hours. With no breaks!"

Just then, the boy rushed past us.

"Where is he going now?" my uncle demanded to know.

"Off to see the king!" said one of the three brothers, rushing after him. "To ask if he can fight the giant!"

"Giant?" asked my uncle. "What giant?"

"That giant!" replied a soldier on the line, pointing across the battlefield.

We looked. There was, indeed, a giant standing there.

"His name's Goliath," the soldier explained. "He is the most powerful and most feared warrior in the Philistine army. He has challenged us to send a champion of our own to fight him. If he wins, we all become his slaves. I thought everybody knew that."

"Some of us are concerned with a more important battle," my uncle proudly proclaimed. "The battle against food poisoning and the odd accidental fall." Then he snapped his fingers. "And if that shepherd boy reaches the king," he said, "there is no telling what damage he might do. Shepherds are not known for their cleanliness. Ticks. Fleas. Who knows what tiny pests that boy is carrying? And if they should hop off onto the king? Well… I think we need to make haste."

So we rushed after the shepherd and his brother, but by the time we reached the king's tent, they had already gone inside.

My uncle was determined, though. He pushed past the king's guards, waving his tablet in their faces and shouting, "Official business! Make way! Must get through!"

And when we burst into the tent, there was the shepherd boy – wearing the king's armour!

"Your Majesty!" cried my uncle. "I must insist that you stop this at once. Fleas! Ticks…!"

"Calm down, soldier," the king commanded. "The boy wants to fight the giant. I'm just giving him a fighting chance."

"But he's not even old enough to serve in the army!" my uncle pleaded.

"He says he's killed a lion and a bear," replied the king. "That takes some doing."

"Begging your pardon, sir," my uncle countered, "we have only his word for this. Now, if he were wearing a bearskin or sporting a lion's pelt…"

"We would definitely have to check for fleas," I whispered.

"Well done, boy," my uncle whispered back. "You're getting the hang of this. You'll most certainly get ahead."

And then the boy dropped the armour on the floor. "Don't need this," he shrugged. "The Lord God helped me defeat the lion and the bear. He'll help me beat the giant, too." Then he pulled a sling out of his belt. "This is all I need. This and a few good stones." And, with that, he marched out of the tent.

"Your Majesty!" my uncle cried again. "That is an unauthorized weapon! It hasn't been tested and certified. You can't let him use that!"

"The boy's got guts," the king nodded. "I'll give him that. And if he wants to face that giant with a sling and a few stones, well… may the Lord God be with him. All I know is that I want to see how this goes." And he marched out of the tent as well.

"Your Majesty," my uncle went on, following behind. "The slingshot may be an appropriate device for farm and field, where the only victim of a badly aimed projectile would be an unfortunate sheep or goat. But a field of battle, crammed with soldiers and their support staff, is no place for such a tool. In short, Your Majesty, HE COULD PUT SOMEBODY'S EYE OUT!"

"Let's hope it's the giant's, then," the king laughed, as we moved to the edge of the battlefield.

The shepherd boy ran toward the giant, and the giant laughed as well. But it was not a nice laugh.

"Do you mock me?" he roared at the Israelites. "Do you think I am a dog? Is that why you send this stick of a boy to fight me? Come closer, lad, and I will feed your flesh to the birds."

"This does not look good," I whispered.

"No," my uncle nodded. "Feeding meat to creatures that are accustomed to eating grain is likely to result in serious health issues."

The boy was not worried, though.

"I come against you in the name of the Lord God of Israel!" he cried. And, placing a stone in his sling, he swung it around his head and let it fly.

"Duck, Your Majesty!" cried my uncle. "The stone could easily come this way."

But it didn't. It hurtled through the air and struck the giant right between the eyes. He fell to the ground at once, and when he did, the shepherd boy ran to his side, grabbed his sword, and cut off his head!

Everyone cheered. The king included. Everyone but my uncle, who tut-tutted and ticked off rows of boxes on his tablet.

"I count seventeen separate violations of our

health and safety codes," he sighed. "It's a miracle that no one was hurt."

"Well, there was the giant," I noted.

And he ticked off another box. "Make that eighteen violations," he added.

And that's when the shepherd boy returned, dragging the giant's head.

"What shall I do with this?" he asked the king.

And the king pointed to my uncle. "Give it to him. He'll know how to dispose of it. Safely, yes?" he chuckled.

"Of course, Your Majesty," my uncle said, bowing. "I would consider it an honour to serve you in this manner."

"See," he winked at me. "I told you this job was the way to get ahead!"

The Widow's Version

Elijah and the Widow

Ever since my dad died, I've sort of had to look out for my mum.

There's the famine, of course. We've been hungry for months, now. More than hungry, actually. Starving.

No sign of rain. Not a cloud in the sky. And no rain means no crops. And no food.

But that's not the only problem with mum.

I mean, I love her. She's amazing. She's kind and caring and everything you'd want your mum to be. But, as my gran says, she is sometimes lacking a bit

in the common-sense department. Especially where men are concerned.

I get it. She needs a man about the house to do the odd job. A handyman. But why does she have to hire so many losers?

There was that guy from Tyre, for example, whose hobby was collecting and preserving strangely shaped sheep droppings. Or whatshisname from Sidon, who would only eat fish that started with the letter A. Or that man from

Gath who insisted that he was the great-great-great-grandson of the giant Goliath. Yeah, right. He was hardly taller than me! Fortunately, they all turned out to be pretty useless – so they didn't last long.

You can imagine my dismay, however, when she came home last week and announced that she'd met yet another man whose

help, she was sure, would be
indispensable.

I sighed. "Where'd you meet
him, Mum?"

"By the city gates," she
answered merrily.

"Not from around here then?"
I asked.

"No. Don't think so," she smiled.
"He's an Israelite."

Do you see what I mean? No common
sense.

"Mum," I said as firmly as I thought I should.
"Mum, we live in Zarephath. We're Phoenicians.
Israelites don't actually like us very much. And
particularly not our religion."

She looked up, as if she was thinking about my
answer. As if she was looking for a reply. And she
was still smiling.

"But didn't our lovely Princess Jezebel marry
Ahab, the Israelite king?"

"Yes, she did," I nodded. "But that was just
politics, Mum. To make a bit of peace. We're still
not what you would call 'fond' of Israelites."

"I don't see why not?" she chirped. "Elijah is a
sweet man – you'll see."

"So his name is Elijah?" I asked. "And his job…?"

"He's a prophet," she replied.

"A prophet?" I repeated.

"Yes, he speaks for God," she smiled.

"The Israelite God?" I queried. "The one who specializes in smiting the Israelites' enemies?"

"That would be the one," she nodded. "And, according to Elijah, he is also the one who is responsible for the drought."

I sat down. This was going to be a long conversation.

"The drought we are currently suffering?" I asked, just a little agitated. "The drought that led to the famine? The famine that led to our present starving situation? The starving situation that will shortly lead to our deaths?"

And again she nodded. "Yes."

"This is the man you have invited to help out around the house?" I cried.

"Yes. Actually, I've invited him to supper tonight," she mumbled. "Well, to share our bread."

"WE HAVE NO BREAD!" I shouted. "Because there is a famine. Because there is a drought. Because the God of your new friend Elijah apparently stopped the rain from falling!"

She shrugged. "Well, when you put it that way, it doesn't sound so nice. But that is still no reason not to give him a chance. After all, he's hungry, too."

"Good," I grunted. "Serves him right."

"I'm not so sure," she went on. "I mean, as long

as the ravens were feeding him, he was fine..."

"Ravens?" I interrupted. "He was fed by ravens?"

"On the far side of the Jordan River," she nodded. "Yes. He says they would bring him bread and meat in the morning, and then more bread and meat at night."

"Mum," I sighed. "Are you sure this guy is a prophet? C'mon. Man Sustained by Sandwich-bearing Birds? He sounds like a nutter to me. Or a liar. Or both."

She patted me on the shoulder. (I hate it when she does that.) And then she said, "I don't care if he's a liar. Or a nutter. Or a prophet. Or even where he comes from. We need the help. He only wants a bit of bread. And I think we should give him some."

My mum. Men. There was no talking to her. I don't even know why I tried.

"All right," I agreed. "Let's scrape together what we've got and make some bread."

So I grabbed the jar of flour. She grabbed the jug of oil. And as she did, she snapped her fingers and smiled again.

"I know you're not going to believe this," she said. "But the prophet told me something else."

I shook my head. "Let me guess. He has a third eye on his elbow? He was raised by whales? He rides about in a chariot made of fire?"

"Nothing as silly as that!" she grinned. "No, when I explained to him that we didn't have much food left, he told me that the God of Israel would make sure that our jar of flour and jug of oil would not run out until the rains began to fall again."

"Still pretty silly," I replied. "Will ravens be filling them then?"

"Let's just make the bread," she said.

So we did. And I know you are going to find this as hard to believe as I did – but I could never get that jar to empty. Or the jug either.

We made Elijah a loaf. And one for ourselves as well. And when we had finished, somehow there was more flour and oil than when we had started!

"Well, Mum," I said. "I've got to hand it to you. He didn't sound promising at first, but I think there might be a future for us and this Elijah fellow."

My mum picked up a piece of camel-shaped sheep poo. "I know you haven't always approved of my choice of handymen," she winked. "But I think I've done all right this time. How about we ask him to stay with us for a while? We could use the help. And, like I always say, it never hurts to have a prophet about the place."

"You've never said that," I sighed.

"Well, I'm saying it now," she replied. And she opened the door and called, "Elijah! Coo-eee! Bread's ready! Come and get it!"

What can I say? I don't always understand her, but I love my mum.

Nigel's Version

The Young Men at the Court of Babylon

The five friends sat nervously together in the hall of the palace.

"What are we doing here?" asked Daniel.

"We're supposed to be slaves, right?" said Hananiah.

"That's what I thought," whispered Mishael. "The Babylonians destroyed Jerusalem and dragged us here to Babylon."

"So why are we in a palace?" wondered Azariah.

And Saul just grunted, "I'm hungry."

Just then a very important-looking man strolled into the room.

"My name is Ashpenaz," he announced. "And I will be in charge of your training."

"Training?" asked Daniel.

And before anyone else could speak, Ashpenaz answered, "That's right, my boy. Training. Or, to be more specific, the very best education that Babylon has to offer."

"But why?" asked Hananiah. "When you destroyed our country and carried our people off as slaves?"

Ashpenaz chuckled. And when he did, his big belly jiggled. And his jowly face as well.

"My dear boy," he began. "We Babylonians are not monsters. You have nothing to fear from us. We are a powerful people, and the destruction of your country is proof of that. But we want you to be happy here. You and all the other Judeans we have brought to work in our fair land. In fact, we want you to become good Babylonians yourselves. You will, after all, be here for a very long time.

"So we will teach you – you, the sons of the finest families from your land – what it means to be Babylonians. And it is our hope that you will come to call our home your home, too. And that all your people here will follow your lead."

"So you want us to forget our country?" asked Mishael.

"And our traditions?" added Azariah.

"It's the only way," smiled Ashpenaz. But it wasn't the friendliest of smiles.

"Is there anything for lunch?" asked Saul.

And now Ashpenaz beamed. "All in good time, my boy. But first, I'd like you to read this." And he handed each boy a little scroll.

"Back in a jiff," he concluded, beaming again at Saul. "And then we'll have a bite to eat."

Daniel read his scroll. "They're giving me a new name," he said. "A Babylonian name. From now on, I'm called Belteshazzar."

"I'm called Shadrach," said Hananiah.

"I'm Meshach," said Mishael.

"Abednego," said Azariah. "And what are they calling you, Saul?" he asked.

And Saul just shrugged and grunted, "I can't quite make it out, but it looks like Nigel."

At that moment, Ashpenaz stuck his head out of a nearby doorway and called, "Dinner's ready, boys. Eat it while it's hot!"

And Belteshazzar, Shadrach, Meshach, Abednego, and Nigel trooped into the dining room.

There were boys from every nation gathered there – from each country that the Babylonians had conquered. And right in the middle stood an empty table, set with five places.

The boys sat down and just stared at the food. It looked amazing. And smelled even better.

"Enjoy!" grinned Ashpenaz. Then he set about chatting with the other boys.

Nigel rubbed his hands together. "About time. And just look at that meat! Let's dig in."

But the others just sat there, motionless.

"You know we can't eat that meat," whispered Belteshazzar.

"I know," Shadrach whispered back. "It's been dedicated to the Babylonian gods."

"And if we eat it," added Meshach, "it's like saying that they're our gods, too."

"And there is only one God," Abednego concluded, "the God of our people, the Maker of heaven and earth."

Meshach

Abednego

Nigel

"C'mon!" cried Nigel. "Enough of the religious stuff! The gravy's getting cold!"

But Belteshazzar had already marched over to Ashpenaz. "I'm sorry," he announced. "But we cannot eat the food you have served us."

"What? Not rich enough for you?" Ashpenaz said in surprise.

"No, it looks amazing," said Belteshazzar. "But there is a problem…" And he explained everything to Ashpenaz.

"I understand your difficulty," Ashpenaz replied. "But if you are going to learn to be good Babylonians, then you will have to eat what Babylonians eat."

"I see," Belteshazzar nodded. And he returned to the table.

"He says we have to eat it," Belteshazzar sighed.

"But we can't," said Shadrach.

"There has to be another way," said Meshach.

"Either that or we starve," added Abednego. "What do you think, Nigel?"

"Mmphhh-mmph," mumbled Nigel, his mouth full of something.

Belteshazzar snapped his fingers. "I've got it!" he announced. "We have a contest. We eat simple food – water and vegetables – stuff that they don't dedicate to their gods. And we show them that we can be even more healthy by doing that!"

"So we teach them something," added Shadrach.

"And we still honour our God!" said Meshach.

"Perfect!" Abednego concluded.

"Are you guys crazy?" Nigel belched. "This grub is incredible! Wake up and smell the sausages!"

Belteshazzar called Ashpenaz over to the table and explained the contest to him. And when he did, every hint of a smile disappeared from Ashpenaz's face.

"This is very unusual," he said. "The king has commanded me to take care of you. If this contest makes you ill, he will have my head."

"Trust us," said Belteshazzar. "At the end of ten days, we will be healthier than any of these other boys."

"And hungrier," mumbled Nigel.

"What was that?" said Abednego.

"Just my tummy grumbling," Nigel replied.

"So you are all agreed on this course of action?" asked Ashpenaz, looking especially hard at Nigel.

"We are!" said Shadrach.

"Then so be it," Ashpenaz agreed. And he ordered the servants to remove everything but vegetables from the table.

"There goes the duck," Nigel sighed. "And the plum sauce. And the roast beef. And the lovely, lovely gravy."

On the first day, all the other boys had...

"Venison," drooled Nigel. "Venison in a wine and pomegranate reduction."

"Eat your broccoli," said Belteshazzar. "It's good for you."

On the second day, all the other boys had...

"Partridge," drooled Nigel. "I don't suppose I could just have one forkful, could I?"

"Not when this turnip stew is so delicious!" chirped Shadrach.

On the third day, all the other boys had...

"Steak!" drooled Nigel. "Thick, fat, juicy steak! Haven't any of you ever heard the saying 'When in Babylon, do what the Babylonians do'?"

"That's a new one to me," mumbled Meshach through a mouthful of sprouts.

And so it continued on the fifth (Camel Chops vs Cabbage), sixth (Fried Chicken vs Beetroot), seventh (Curried Lamb vs Leek), and eighth (Hunter's Pie vs Lettuce) days… so that by the ninth day, Nigel could hardly control himself.

"I don't care!" he cried, as all the other boys dug into their roast beef. "Surely it's important to

respect the way that other people live, and to learn to appreciate what's good about it. It's all about tasting… yes, tasting – that's the perfect word – tasting those differences for ourselves! We shouldn't be bound by what our parents or our religions say, but free to decide for ourselves."

"An open-minded viewpoint," grinned Ashpenaz, who happened to be wandering by. "Very admirable, my boy," he added, dangling a juicy bit of beef in front of Nigel's face.

"Don't do it!" pleaded Belteshazzar. "They want us to forget everything that's important to us – our home, our history, our God!"

"Nonsense," grinned Ashpenaz. "We just want you to be exactly like us." Then he dipped the beef into the gravy boat. And that's when Nigel snapped.

He grabbed the beef and the gravy, dashed off to one of the other tables, and stuffed himself until he could hardly breathe.

"Day ten tomorrow," sneered Ashpenaz. "Then we'll see who is happy and who is healthy, and who is not."

When the morning came, Ashpenaz called the five friends to stand before him.

"And how are we feeling today?" he asked. "Ready at last for a big Babylonian breakfast?"

"No thanks," said Belteshazzar. "I'm feeling fine."

"Me too," said Shadrach.

"Couldn't be better," added Meshach.

"Healthy and happy and fit!" chirped Abednego.

And all the servants and guards and other officials had to agree.

"The king will be pleased," one of them said. "You have done a brilliant job with these newcomers, Ashpenaz. They are in better shape than any of the other boys!"

"And what about your friend?" Ashpenaz asked. "Surely he is better still?"

"No, he's not," said Belteshazzar. "He's been up all night. As sick as a dog."

And so it was that Belteshazzar, Shadrach, Meshach, and Abednego were blessed by the God they would not forget. They became famous for their intelligence, their wisdom, and their courage.

And Nigel?

All he got was a really bad tummy.

The Lion's Version

Daniel in the Lions' Den

It's tough being a lion. And I'm not lion.

Lion? Get it? Lyin'. Sorry.

That's the problem. Nobody expects a lion to have a sense of humour. We're supposed to be fierce and proud and obsessed with tearing things to bits. And, fair enough, some lions are.

Take my sister, for example. She'd sooner bite the head off a bunny than look at it. You just don't mess with her. Particularly at dinner time.

But me? I'm just put together differently, I guess. I'll let the odd bunny past. No problem. Antelopes, just the same. Sure, I like a good meal now and

then. Who doesn't? Circle of life and all that. But I'm not looking to devour everyone in the room or kill the first thing that moves. I'd rather just lie in the sun and enjoy the moment.

That's what I was doing, in fact, when they dropped this old guy into my living space.

When I say "living space", I mean the place where my sister and I hang out. It's not in the wild as it used to be when we were cubs. It's smaller. There's an "outside" bit with rocks to lie on and an "inside" bit that's covered, for when it rains. A den.

And when I say "they", I mean the men who took us from the wild to this place and who drop food down into our living space from time to time.

My sister hates this arrangement. As I said, she enjoys the hunting thing and is generally quite grumpy anyway. Me? I love it! Free food. Regular naps. What more could a lion ask for?

Anyway, this old guy dropped down into the den one day, and at first I wasn't quite sure what to do.

My sister, of course, was all roar and fang and claw.

"Calm down," I told her. "Let's think this thing through."

"What's to think about?" she growled. "He dropped down. He's dinner!"

All instinct, my sister. All the time.

"But look at him," I said. "There's no meat on

those bones. What kind of dinner is that? I think this is a mistake. I say he's actually one of the dinner-droppers and that he FELL down. And if we eat him, we might make the other dinner-droppers mad."

"So?" she grunted.

"So," I argued, "they might not feed us again. Not if we've eaten one of them."

"But how do we find out?" she replied. "It's not as if we can ask them."

"We wait," I said, "and see if they come back for him. Look, he's on his knees. He's staring up in the air. And he's saying something. Maybe he's calling for help."

"But I'm hungry," she grumbled.

"You're always hungry," I grumbled back. "How about we wait until it's dark? If they don't come back by then, we'll know that they meant to feed him to us. And, fine, you can eat whatever meat you can pick off those bones of his."

Then I went back to my rock and fell asleep.

When I woke up, the sun was setting, the old guy was still kneeling, and my sister was drooling.

"Any minute now," she smiled.

"Whatever," I shrugged. "There's been plenty of time for them to come back for him."

And then somebody else dropped in.

I say "dropped in". I suppose I really mean "appeared".

He wasn't there and then he was. Bit like a meerkat, popping up out of hole. But there was no hole. And he was bigger than a meerkat. Lots bigger.

My sister, of course, decided that he would make a much better dinner than the old guy in the corner. So she leaped in his direction, claws bared, fangs flashing. Big Mistake.

First, she flew right through him! I am not making this up. It was as if he was made of air. Whoosh!

"Might want to rethink this, Sis," I suggested. But the adrenalin was flowing. And the blood lust. She's an animal – what can I say?

So she leaped again. And this time, he was as solid as a rock – and she bounced off him with a whimper and a thud.

"Sis," I sighed, "leave it. You're not gonna eat that one."

"Then I'll have the old man," she growled.

"No, you won't," said the newcomer. And my sister and I just looked at each other.

"Did you hear that?" I whispered.

"I did," she whispered back.

"Not a man then," I said. "They can't understand us."

"What then?" she replied.

And our visitor smiled and said, "An angel."

It was, I must admit, a new concept to me. Not

man. Not lion. Not meerkat. So I asked him to explain.

"I am a servant of the Most High God," he said, "who is the Maker of All Things."

Now this I understood. In fact, I found it quite comforting. I would often lie on my rock, staring up into the sky. Clouds in the day. Stars at night. My sister thought I was lazy. But I was actually thinking. And one of the things I'd thought was, "This can't all be here by chance. Somebody must have made it." And here was the proof.

But my sister? She just grunted, "So what?"

"So," the angel answered, "I have been sent by the Maker of All Things to protect Daniel – the man over there."

"Because…?" I asked. I was on a roll, thinking-wise.

"Because he has followed the Maker faithfully, praying to him daily."

"Praying…?" I asked again.

"Talking to the Maker," the angel explained. "And, for that, a king called Darius, who rules this land, has said that he must die. And he has ordered his men to leave him here for you to eat."

"Sounds like a plan to me," grinned my sister.

"Wait a minute," I said. "This Darius wants him dead just because he talked to the Maker? I don't get it."

"To be fair," the angel explained, "the king does

not want him to die. He was tricked into this by his advisors – men who are jealous of Daniel. They are the ones who want him dead."

"And they call us animals," I sighed. "We only kill to eat."

"And, speaking of eating…" added my sister.

"Yes, yes, I see the dilemma," said the angel. "You want to eat Daniel. I need to protect him. How about this? What if we wait until morning?"

"Morning?" moaned my sister.

"Wait until morning," the angel continued. "And I promise you the biggest meal you've ever had."

My sister looked sceptical. "The biggest? Really?"

"Really!" the angel grinned. "I promise."

"Say you'll wait, Sis," I whispered. "You've already tried to get past him. It's the only choice you've got."

"All right," she sighed, "Might as well go to sleep then." And she curled up into a ball.

I went back to my rock. And the angel? Who knows? He was awake the next morning when I woke up. My sister was awake, too, waiting for her breakfast. And so was somebody else.

"It's King Darius," the angel explained, as a head peeped over the edge of our den. And then the head said something.

"What's he going on about?" I asked.

"He wants to know if Daniel is still alive," the angel translated, while Daniel shouted and jumped up and down.

"I take it that means 'yes'," I chuckled.

"Good call," the angel chuckled in return. "And now the king is saying how pleased he is, and that

Daniel's god must be the true god if he could save him from a den of hungry lions."

"Yes. Hungry," my sister interrupted. "What about that promise of yours?"

"Hold on," said the angel. "Ah, yes, here it comes. King Darius says that Daniel will now be set free. Look, there's the rope. And there he goes. And – wait for it – the evil advisors who were jealous of Daniel will now be condemned to take his place. And here they come!"

My sister's eyes were as big as saucers, for the three men who dropped down into the den were the fattest three men either of us had ever seen!

"Lots of meat on those bones," I said.

"King's advisors eat well," nodded the angel.

"Breakfast time!" roared my sister. And, well, do you really want me to describe what happened next? Suffice to say that it was, as promised, the biggest meal she'd ever had.

"Farewell," said the angel.

"Fangs. Fangs a lot," I replied. "Get it? Fangs. Fanks. Thanks."

That's all right – the angel didn't laugh either. He just rolled his eyes and did his meerkat disappearing act. First he was there. Then he was gone. Back to the Maker of All Things.

And (heh heh) I'm not lion!

Also by Bob Hartman

Bible Baddies
More Bible Baddies
Stories from the Stable
The Lion Storyteller Easter Book
New Testament Tales: The Unauthorized Version

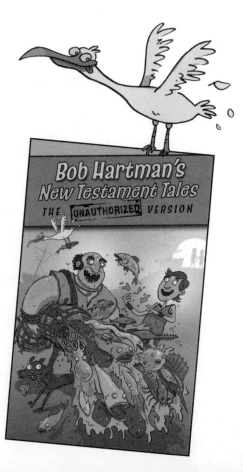